Contents

Childhood

Grace Darling was brought up in a lighthouse. Her father, William, had grown up in a lighthouse as well, because his father was the light-keeper. Their lighthouse was on Brownsman Island.

William had worked as a boat boy, rowing supplies and people across the sea between the islands. After he married, he became his father's assistant light-keeper.

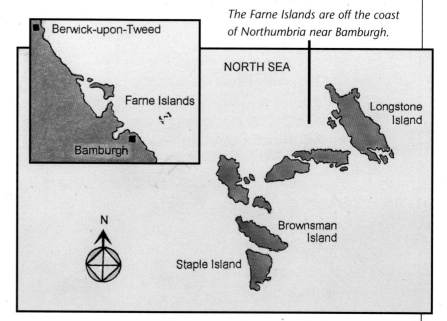

The Farne Islands are off the coast of Northumbria near Bamburgh.

William and his wife, Thomasin, had nine children. Their seventh child, Grace, was born in 1815 on 24 November.

This is the cradle in which baby Grace slept.

Famous People

GRACE DARLING

1815 ~ 1842

Christine Moorcroft

Magnus Magnusson

Christine Moorcroft is an educational consultant and an Ofsted inspector, who was a teacher in primary and special schools and a lecturer in education. She has written and edited several books on history and religion and on other subjects, including personal and social education, science and English.

Magnus Magnusson KBE, has written several books on history and archaeology, and translated many Icelandic sagas and modern Icelandic novels. He has presented major television programmes on history and archaeology, such as *Chronicle*, *The Archaeology of the Bible Lands* and *Living Legends*, as well as the long-running quiz series, *Mastermind*. He is currently chairman of Scottish Natural Heritage, the Government body which advises on environmental issues.

ACKNOWLEDGEMENTS

The authors thank Christine Bell, Honorary Curator, Grace Darling
Museum, Bamburgh, for her help.

Picture credits
All photographs © Colin Dixon except for: page 6 © J Allan Cash and
page 8 © Tessa Bunney

Illustrations Rodney Sutton

Published by Channel Four Learning Limited
Castle House
75–76 Wells Street
London W1P 3RE

© 1998 Channel Four Learning

Written by Christine Moorcroft and Magnus Magnusson
Illustrated by Rodney Sutton
Cover illustration by Jeffrey Burn
Designed by Blade Communications
Edited by Margot O'Keeffe
Printed by Alden Press
ISBN 1-86215-347-7

For further information about Channel 4 Schools and details of
published materials, contact
Channel 4 Schools
PO Box 100
Warwick CV34 6TZ
Tel: 01926 436444
Fax: 01926 436446

William Darling taught all his children to read, write and do mathematics. He also taught them about geography and history.

When they were 11 years old, the boys went to a school in Bamburgh Castle. Grace and her sisters learned to knit, spin, sew and cook and, like all lighthouse-keepers' children, they helped to look after the lighthouse.

There was no bathroom in Grace's home. She would fill this big jug with water and take it to her bedroom. The bowl was her washbasin.

Did you know?

- *For hundreds of years there have been lights or fires to warn sailors of dangerous rocks.*

- *In 1795, the first lighthouse on Brownsman Island burned coal and wood.*

- *In 1810, the tower was rebuilt and a new light, which burned oil, was put in. It turned by clockwork so that the light flashed.*

5

Life on Brownsman Island

Grace and her family were given a free home in return for working in the lighthouse. They helped to look out for ships and took turns to make sure the light did not go out.

Oil for the light and food for the family, such as flour, smoked pork and bacon, came from the mainland. They kept rabbits and sheep for meat and goats for milk, and they grew vegetables.

Mr Darling shot wild ducks to eat (mallard, teal and wigeon). They also caught fish and collected sea birds' eggs.

Ruins of the old lighthouse on Brownsman Island. This was Grace's first home.

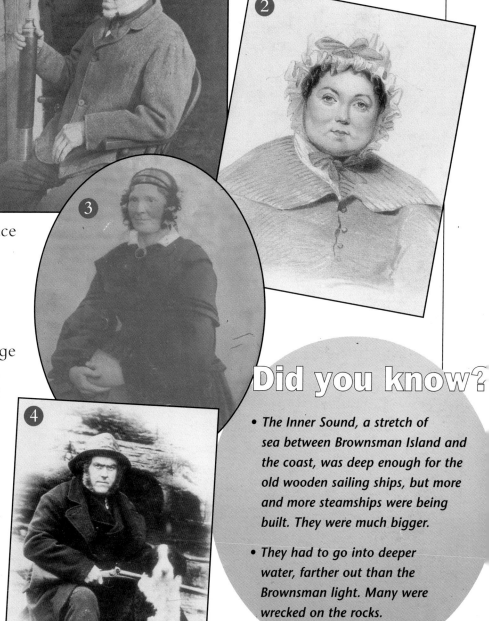

It was very crowded in the little cottage. When Grace was born, there was her brother William, who was nine, and twin girls, Thomasin and Mary, who were seven. Then there was Job, who was four, Elizabeth Grace who was three and Robert, who was only one year old.

When Grace was three, her twin brothers, George Alexander and William Brooks, were born. Her elder brother, Job, died when he was only 19.

Sometimes the family had paying guests from the mainland.

These photos are of:
1. Grace's father, William Darling.
2. Her mother, Thomasin Darling.
3. Grace's sister, Thomasin.
4. George Alexander, her brother.

Did you know?

- The Inner Sound, a stretch of sea between Brownsman Island and the coast, was deep enough for the old wooden sailing ships, but more and more steamships were being built. They were much bigger.

- They had to go into deeper water, farther out than the Brownsman light. Many were wrecked on the rocks.

7

Longstone lighthouse

When Grace was ten years old the family moved to a new home. A new lighthouse had been built on Longstone Island. There were often fierce gales here and sometimes the sea washed right over the island!

The family lived in the lighthouse itself. All the rooms were round and on top of one another! Rainwater was stored in underground tanks for washing. Like everyone else at the time, they used candles and oil-lamps for light.

The kitchen/living room in the lighthouse was circular. It measured nearly six metres across. The bedrooms had bunks built into the walls.

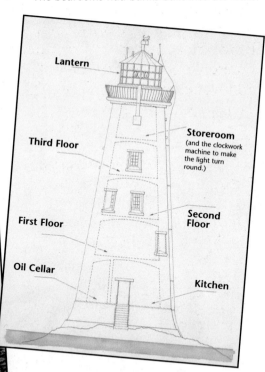

Lantern

Third Floor

First Floor

Oil Cellar

Storeroom
(and the clockwork machine to make the light turn round.)

Second Floor

Kitchen

The Longstone Lighthouse in the Farne Islands as it looks today.

The Farne Islands are famous for their eider ducks. Grace fed the ducks and talked to them. They were not afraid of her and one would even let her get close to its nest.

Mrs Darling made quilts which she filled with eiderdown – the soft feathers of eider ducks.

Every day, Mr Darling or one of the older children would row across to Brownsman Island to look after their vegetable garden and the animals and sometimes to bring back food.

A painting of the Darling family in the kitchen/living room of the Longstone Lighthouse.

Did you know?

- *The new lighthouse had to be built on one of the farthest islands from the coast to warn the big steamships of the dangers of rocks.*

- *It was ready in February 1826, and on 18 February the old Brownsman light was put out. It was no longer needed.*

9

The work of a lighthouse-keeper and his family

A portrait of Grace when she was a young woman.

By the time Grace was 19 years old all but one of her brothers and sisters had left home to marry or to work on the mainland. Only she and her 16-year-old brother, William Brooks, stayed.

Every day their father had to polish the brass reflectors and clean the lamps and the windows of the lighthouse lantern. He had to check the wicks and make sure there was enough oil in the lamps. He also had to make sure the lighthouse was kept in good repair. Grace and her brother helped him.

Grace also helped her mother with the housework and cooking and she made shirts for her father and her unmarried brothers.

As well as this, she helped to mend the fishing nets and spread herrings on the rocks to dry in the sun. Sometimes Grace's father and brother needed her help to collect salvage from wrecked ships.

Although she was busy, Grace found time, with her father, to learn about the birds and plants of the Farne Islands and to collect sea shells.

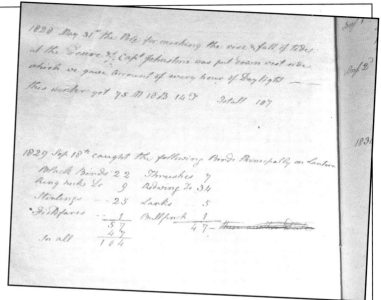

A page from a notebook in which Grace's father kept information about the birds on the island.

Did you know?

- Nowadays, the lights in lighthouses are worked automatically, so there is no need for lighthouse-keepers like Grace's father.

The wreck of the Forfarshire

On Wednesday 5 September 1838, a ship called the *Forfarshire* set off from Hull to Dundee in Scotland. It was carrying a cargo of cloth, hardware and soap. There were also 63 passengers and crew.

The next morning, the ship's boiler began to leak. After a while hot water slopped about and scalding steam filled the air in the boiler room. The men could not get near the furnace. By this time the ship was north of the Farne Islands and the weather was bad.

At 1 o'clock in the morning on 7 September the engine stopped. There was no power to drive it, and the *Forfarshire* began to drift helplessly. The crew hoisted the sails and tried to steer the ship.

Then the weather got worse. The passengers had stayed below deck to shelter from the heavy rain and gusts of wind, so they could not see the huge waves crashing over the decks.

The captain struggled to steer the ship towards the Inner Sound which was sheltered by the islands from the open sea.

Suddenly there was a great crash as the *Forfarshire* struck a rock. There was no time to call the passengers from their cabins and get them into the boats.

A plate from the Forfarshire, showing a picture of the ship.

Did you know?

- *The Forfarshire was one of the first British paddle steamers.*

- *The first-class passengers had a saloon with painted wall panels and marble mantelpieces. They had silver cutlery and china crockery and slept in comfortable cabins.*

- *It was not so comfortable for steerage passengers who sat, and slept, on wooden benches.*

13

A stormy night

On the night of 6 September, 1838, only Grace and her parents were in the lighthouse. The stone walls were so thick that they may not have heard the howling wind and the crashing waves.

When her father went to check the lamp at midnight, he could tell there was going to be a fierce storm. Everything outside had to be tied down or brought indoors. He asked Grace to help him.

Together they managed to make everything safe. First, they lashed their coble (a small rowboat) more securely to its iron rings and tied down its oars. Then they brought into the kitchen the rabbits in their hutch, the nets, the washing basket and other small things.

Once everything was safe they went back indoors tired, cold and soaking wet.

Above is the Darling family's rowboat. It was named after Grace and is now in the Grace Darling Museum.

Grace was still awake at 4.45am. She looked out of the window at the storm. Something looked different. What was that black mass? It was a ship! Grace ran up to the lantern to get a better view. Yes, surely it was a ship on the rocks. She hurried to wake her father.

They strained their eyes in the mist and darkness to see if anyone was still on the wreck. At nearly 7am it was light enough to see that someone was moving on the rocks.

Mr Darling did not think that the lifeboats on the mainland would be able to put to sea in such a storm. There were lives to be saved. He would have to go himself, and the only one who could help him was Grace.

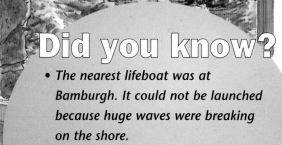

Did you know?

- *The nearest lifeboat was at Bamburgh. It could not be launched because huge waves were breaking on the shore.*

- *The North Sunderland lifeboat could not be launched either, but the lifeboatmen there were able to launch a rowing boat.*

15

The rescue

Grace and her father set out in their boat to help the survivors. It was a struggle for them in a boat which needed at least three people to row it in rough seas!

When they reached the survivors, they saw that there were at least nine people; their boat could only carry seven.

Grace's father realised that the only way he could land safely was to wait for the next wave and then leap on to the rock. This left Grace to handle the boat alone. To keep it in one place she had to take both oars and row backwards and forwards.

A painting of the Wreck of the Forfarshire.

16

On the rock, Mr Darling found eight men, one of whom was badly injured. There was also a woman holding her two children, who were both dead. There was also a dead man.

Mr Darling and three of the men rowed the boat back to the lighthouse. They took with them Grace, the injured man and the woman. Then they went back to fetch the other four survivors.

Mrs Darling was waiting at Longstone with a roaring fire, hot food and dry clothes for everyone.

Then at 11am, the crew of the North Sunderland lifeboat arrived! They had managed to put to sea in a rowing boat but had found only the dead man and children on the rock. They went to the Longstone lighthouse to shelter. Imagine their surprise when they found it crowded with people!

This Victorian illustration shows the Darlings and the people they rescued in the lighthouse.

Did you know?

- *The survivors were stranded on a big rock called Big Harcar.*

- *The shortest route from Longstone to Big Harcar rock was across the open sea and was nearly 870m.*

- *Because their little boat could not go out into the open sea in the gale, Grace and her father had to go the long route, around the rocks. This route was 1.6 km.*

Heroes

News spread of the bravery of Grace and her father. People began to arrive at the Farne Islands to see them. They wrote to Grace asking for locks of her hair. They sent her presents. Men even wrote asking her to marry them!

She was offered a role in a play in London called *Wreck at Sea*. But Grace refused. She did not think of herself as a heroine.

Special tins of chocolates were made to commemorate the event.

People wanted to reward the Darlings. £725 was collected for Grace, and £175 for her father. William Wordsworth wrote a poem about the rescue.

A VISIT TO THE HEROINE

GRACE HORSLEY DARLING, At the Longstone Island.

The Public are respectfully informed the

TWEEDSIDE

Will leave the Folly Wharf, Newcastle, on Whit-Monday, at half-past 6, and the New Quay, North Shields, at 8 o'Clock, having on board an experienced Holy Island Pilot, to conduct the Party to that interesting Family whose Names are now Immortalized; and after going round the Romantic Groups of the Ferns will proceed to Berwick, returning next Morning at 9, calling at the Ferns and North Sunderland.

A Steward and Stewardess to attend to the Comfort of the Passengers. An efficient Boat and Crew for convenience of Landing. FARE, THERE AND BACK, FIVE SHILLINGS.

North Shields, May 11th, 1839. W. ORANGE, PRINTER.

This poster advertised a day trip to visit Grace Darling.

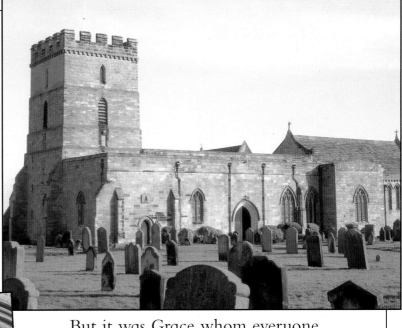

St Aidan's churchyard, Bamburgh, where Grace Darling is buried.

Nine other people had survived the wreck. When the *Forfarshire* struck the rocks the stern of the ship had broken off and was swept away. Eight of the crew and one passenger managed to scramble into the ship's lifeboat and were rescued.

Grace Darling's memorial.

But it was Grace whom everyone remembered. Sadly, she became ill with tuberculosis a few years later, in 1842. She went to stay with her sister Thomasin, in Bamburgh, where she died when she was only 26. Her grave is in St Aidan's churchyard in Bamburgh.

Did you know?

- **The wreck of the Forfarshire was reported in many newspapers.**

- **Grace herself wrote letters about it. Members of her family have kept them.**

Time-lines

Grace Darling was born

Work began on the new Longstone lighthouse

1815

1825 1826

The Darling family moved from Brownsman Island to Longstone Island

55
Julius Caesar invaded Britain

c30
Jesus was crucified

c570
Muhammad was born

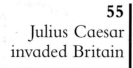

500BC

0

AD500

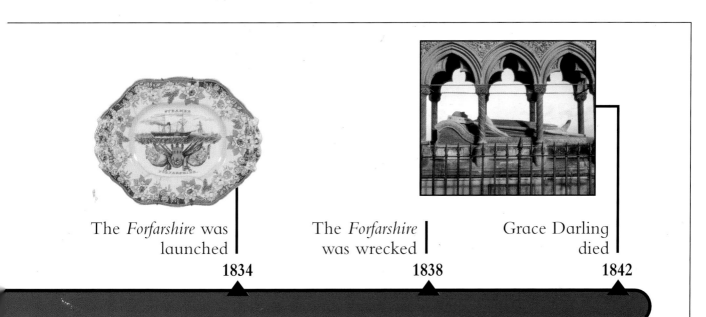

The *Forfarshire* was launched
1834

The *Forfarshire* was wrecked
1838

Grace Darling died
1842

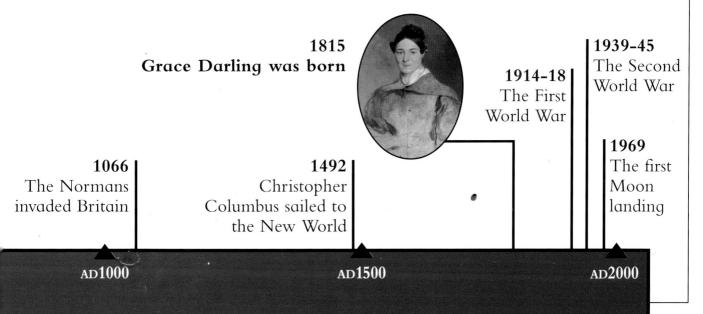

1815
Grace Darling was born

1066
The Normans invaded Britain

AD1000

1492
Christopher Columbus sailed to the New World

AD1500

1914–18
The First World War

1939–45
The Second World War

1969
The first Moon landing

AD2000

How to find out more

More books to read

Birds of the Farne Islands by Peter Hawkey
(Butler Publishing, 1990)

The Story of Grace Darling by Helen Cresswell
(Viking Kestrel, 1988)

The Farne Islands by M Scott Weightman
(M S Weightman, 1988)

Grace Darling by W A Montgomery & M Scott
Weightman (M S Weightman, 1974)

Rescue Call by Angus MacVicar (Kaye & Ward,
1967)

Grace Darling: Maid and Myth by Richard Armstrong
(G M Dent & Sons, 1965)

Grace Darling: The Heroine of the Farne Islands
by Eva Hope (Walter Scott)

Eight Famous Lifeboat Rescues by Len Ortzen (Arthur
Barker)

Grace Darling and her Times by Constance Smedley
(Hurst & Blackett, 1932). There is a copy of this
book in the Grace Darling Museum.

Television programmes to watch

Channel 4 Schools series, Stop Look, Listen:
Famous People. Telephone 01926 436444.

Newspaper reports to read

(from local libraries)

| *The Berwick Advertiser* | (15 September, 1938) |
| *The Newcastle Chronicle* | (15 September, 1938) |

A cassette to play

Grace Darling: Story & Songs by Christine Bell
(The Grace Darling Museum, 1997)

Places to visit

Grace Darling's birthplace, Bamburgh.

Grace Darling Museum, Radcliffe Road,
Bamburgh NE69 7AE. Tel 01668 214465.

Longstone Lighthouse, Farne Islands.

St Aidan's Church, Radcliffe Road, Bamburgh.

Places to which to write

Corporation of Trinity House, Trinity House,
Tower Hill, London EC3N 4DH.
Tel 0171 480 6601.

Royal National Lifeboat Institution,
West Quay Road, Poole, Dorset BH15 1HZ.
Tel 01202 633000.

Glossary

cabin *(13)* A room in which people sleep on a ship.

cargo *(12)* Goods carried on a ship.

coble *(14)* A small flat-bottomed fishing boat used in the North of England.

crew *(12)* A group of people who work on a ship or boat.

eider duck *(9)* A duck whose down is used for filling eiderdowns.

eiderdown *(9)* A kind of quilt or duvet, filled with the soft down (breast feathers) of eider ducks.

furnace *(12)* A big fire which is used for heating things like the boilers in ships and trains.

mallard *(6)* A wild duck.

paddle steamer *(13)* A ship powered by a steam engine which turns huge paddle wheels.

reflector *(10)* Something with a shiny surface to reflect light.

salvage *(11)* Things saved from accidents like shipwrecks, floods and fires.

saloon *(13)* A room on a ship or in a building where people can go to sit and buy drinks and snacks.

steerage *(13)* The part of the ship below the decks where passengers who paid the cheapest fares slept.

stern *(19)* The back part of a ship.

teal *(6)* A wild duck.

tuberculosis (TB) *(19)* A disease which harms people's lungs. It was called 'consumption' in Grace Darling's time. Many people died from it then but nowadays it is rare.

wick *(10)* The part of an oil lamp or candle which burns.

wigeon *(6)* A wild duck.

Index